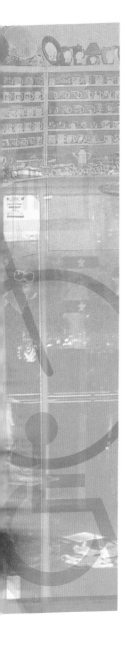

...you. A survey of consumer rights, however, is only a start. No book could cover the topic in a comprehensive manner or even exhaust the issues of a particular subject. Understanding Consumer Rights will, however, provide you with many tips and tools to protect and control your own life—from purchases to privacy. The topics inside reflect broad consumer concerns and often raise consumer questions. It's important to note that laws and regulations change and are subject to interpretation by agencies, administrative proceedings, and courts. You shouldn't consider or rely on the information presented here as legal advice. It's intended for informational purposes only. You can become a more confident and savvy consumer by understanding the issues that confront you every day.

GETTING STARTED

To begin, you should know what types of rights are available to you, where your rights originate, and who protects your rights.

AT THE BEGINNING

This overview will help you understand the foundations of your consumer rights and be prepared as those rights evolve in the future.

THE FOUNDATION OF CONSUMER RIGHTS

The movement to provide consumer rights can, in part, be traced to the development of product liability laws in the 1950s. The concept behind product liability is that a manufacturer is liable if the evidence shows that its defective product caused an injury.

Consumer rights have also come from various campaigns waged by consumer advocacy groups. Although the Consumers Union was formed in 1936, most advocacy groups stem from individual and community action activities in the 1960s and 1970s. For example, Ralph Nader published *Unsafe at Any Speed* in 1965 and founded the *Public Citizen* in 1971. Both events raised awareness of vehicle safety as a consumer issue. Today, many groups focus on consumer issues and fight for your rights.

IT'S A FACT

In 1962, President John F. Kennedy highlighted consumer issues in a message to Congress, and raised public awareness.

IT'S A FACT

In the 1970s, federal laws were enacted to address many consumer issues that affect your daily life.

CAVEAT EMPTOR

Caveat emptor is a Latin phrase that means "let the buyer beware." The buyer bears the risk of a transaction without recourse or remedy for unforeseen or hidden problems that the consumer might discover later. In the 20th century, federal and state legislation altered that equation in purchasing, financing, investing, privacy, insurance, and other areas. While *caveat emptor* is always a good concept to keep in mind, today's consumer protection laws ensure buyers are not entirely at the mercy of sellers and manufacturers.

CORNERSTONES OF CONSUMER RIGHTS

Here are the cornerstones of consumer rights:

DISCLOSURE LAWS
The adage that "knowledge is power" is particularly true for consumers, and knowledge is the basic element of consumer rights. Your knowledge comes from laws that require information to be disclosed (told) to consumers before they make a decision.

GOVERNMENT OVERSIGHT
Consumer rights laws also incorporate government oversight of manufacturers, sellers, lenders, and others. Congress and state legislatures ensure compliance with laws intended to protect consumers by authorizing an agency to regulate and enforce the law and regulations.

LEGAL REMEDIES
There are laws that provide remedies to consumers. These laws—both federal and state—go a step beyond your right to be told; they give you tools to address problems.

YOUR RESPONSIBILITIES
The final cornerstone is you. It's ultimately up to you, the consumer, to take the right steps. Exercise your rights in order to protect yourself and ensure that you receive all the benefits to which you're entitled.

BUYER'S RIGHTS

Today, consumers have more information, options, and remedies than ever before.

CREDIT RIGHTS

A consumer's credit rights are based on disclosure of information and the right to dispute errors.

DISCLOSURES PRIOR TO A LOAN

The federal Truth in Lending Act ensures that consumers have information that allows comparison of credit offers. It says that creditors must provide the terms and costs of all loan plans, including:

- Finance charges and annual percentage rate (APR);
- The source of the credit and the amount of the credit line;
- The grace period, if any, before payment is required;
- The minimum payment and when payments are due;
- Annual fees, if any;
- Late payment fees.

 If you're denied credit, you're legally entitled to know the reason for the denial.

CORRECTING ERRORS

If you find an error on an ATM statement or receipt, you only have 60 days to notify the bank. The bank has 10 days (up to 45 days if it needs more time and recredits the disputed amount to your account) to investigate and give you the results.

BILLING DISPUTES

The Fair Credit Billing Act addresses billing errors on credit cards, revolving charge accounts, and overdraft checking accounts. The law doesn't apply to installment contracts such as automobile loans, or extensions of credit repaid on a fixed schedule. Billing errors include purchases you returned or never received, duplicate charges, and failures to record your payment. They don't include complaints about the quality of goods.

What you do. To dispute a billing error, you must write to the creditor at its "billing inquiries" address and include identifying information and copies of receipts. The letter must be received within 60 days after the first bill showing the error. You can withhold payment of the disputed amount but not the part of the bill that isn't in dispute.

What creditors do. The creditor must acknowledge your letter within 30 days and resolve your dispute within two billing cycles (not more than 90 days) after receiving your letter. Your credit rating can't be affected while disputing a bill. If, after investigation, you do owe the creditor, you will have to pay the applicable interest charges in addition to the disputed amount.

2 A bank can't take money from your checking account to cover a missed credit card payment.

LOST OR STOLEN CARDS

Credit cards. If your credit card is lost or stolen, federal laws limit your liability for unauthorized use of a credit card to $50. Ask the issuer of your card whether it will waive even that amount.

ATM or debit card. The Electronic Fund Transfer Act provides that your liability for unauthorized use of a debit card will be:

- $0 (if you report the card missing before it's used);
- Up to $50 (if you notify the bank within two business days of realizing the card is missing);
- Up to $500 (if you notify the bank more than two days but within 60 days after your bank statement is mailed);
  - Unlimited (if you don't notify the bank within 60 days after your bank statement is mailed).

CANCELLING A PURCHASE

W*hat if you decide that you don't really want to buy that vacuum or join that health club? For consumer goods, there may be a window for you to change your mind. This is called the cooling-off period.*

FEDERAL COOLING-OFF PERIODS

Cooling-off laws were passed to help consumers fight high-pressure sales tactics and change their minds after considering their decision away from the salesperson. The federal cooling-off rule allows you to cancel a contract up to midnight on the third business day after you've signed a contract for:

- Door-to-door purchases of more than $25;
- Sales of more than $25 at other than the merchant's place of business;
- A home improvement loan, second mortgage, or other loan with your home as security (except for a first mortgage).

DON'T LET ▶ THEM TWIST YOUR ARM
Salespeople can be very persuasive. You may, however, have the right to change your mind later.

STATE COOLING-OFF PERIODS

Many states have their own laws with different cooling-off periods. The time period for cancellation depends on the state and type of contract. Here are some examples of types of contracts that may have cooling-off periods:

- Credit repair and home improvement contracts;
- Dating services, seminar sales, and discount buying services;
- Vacation timeshare contracts;
- Dance studios, dental services, and health club memberships;
- Rent-to-own agreements, hearing aids, and certain immigration consultant services;
- Home water-softening equipment that's sold, rented or leased. In some states, it's considered to be a home solicitation contract.

3 Be certain the salesperson records the correct date and time on all copies of the signed contract.

OTHER RULES

Cancellation of special orders is a special situation. If the retailer has "special ordered" the item for you, know your cancellation rights in advance. The merchant may be stuck with the item if you change your mind. To avoid being left holding special-ordered goods, the merchant can ask for a non-refundable deposit.

The cooling-off periods usually include Monday through Saturday but Sundays and most holidays are excluded. The day ends at midnight, local time. This is important if you decide to cancel at the last moment. Many contracts will identify the date and time of the approval to start the clock for the cancellation window. If you receive notice of the cooling-off period at a later time, then your cancellation window begins when you receive the notice. You don't have to explain why you're cancelling a purchase.

The seller has ten days after you cancel to return:
- Any promissory note;
- Your money;
- Any trade-in.

You must return the goods in the condition you received them or you will have to pay for them.

READ INSTRUCTIONS

When you sign a contract for products or services, note any written instruction on how to cancel. These instructions tell the consumer how to cancel, where to send a cancellation letter, or who to call to cancel over the phone, and sometimes it will give you the name of the person authorized to accept the cancellation. If you follow these instructions, you're more likely to avoid any problems later.

CANCELLATION CHECKLIST

Here's a checklist to help guide you through the cancellation process:
- Keep a detailed record of whom you spoke with, what was agreed upon, and the terms of any refund coming to you;
- Send the cancellation notice by first class mail, return receipt requested;
- Write down the full name and phone number of any person you speak with at the company;
- Keep original documents and receipts and only mail copies;
- Follow the directions on how to cancel so you don't lose your rights to sue in small claims court or if the company sues you.

WARRANTIES

Warranties (also called guarantees) represent the obligation of the seller or manufacturer to you. For the period of the warranty, the seller/manufacturer stands behind the product and you have remedies if the product fails.

FEDERAL LAW

The federal law that addresses consumer product warranties was passed in 1975. The purpose of the law was to ensure that you're informed about warranties before buying a product and have the opportunity to compare the terms and conditions of different product warranties.

This federal law doesn't require a business to provide a written warranty and doesn't apply to:

- Oral warranties;
- Products for resale or for commercial purposes; or,
- Warranties on services.

If a business decides to provide a written warranty for consumer goods, then the law's provisions apply.

ENFORCING A WARRANTY

The retailer is the first line of defense for the warranty. If the problem occurs shortly after purchase, a retailer may offer to fix or replace the product or refund the cost. After this time, you must deal with the manufacturer or a third-party repair company.

Mail or Internet orders. You may be required to return the product at your cost with full packaging for a refund. After the initial period, usually 5-30 days, you may only be able to get the product repaired.

After it's yours. You can withhold payment (or refuse to pay your credit card) if the manufacturer doesn't repair a product that's under warranty. If you've already paid, you may want to consider complaint resolution programs, such as the Better Business Bureau program, which helps to mediate these types of problems.

Legal action. If you decide that you want to sue because the product wasn't repaired, be sure to check your state's timeframe to bring a lawsuit (called the *statute of limitations*).

EXPRESS WARRANTIES

Express warranties are promises that back up a product in the manner stated by the manufacturer or seller. The statement is either in writing or by oral agreement. Typically an express warranty is limited in time—one year, five years, or another specific timeframe. You're not entitled to receive an express warranty. There are two types of express warranties.

Full. A full warranty is a promise to repair or replace a product during the warranty period without charge. If the item can't be repaired, a replacement or refund must be offered.

Limited. A limited warranty may cover only certain parts (not labor).

IMPLIED WARRANTIES

Unless a product you're purchasing is marked "as is," it's generally covered by an implied warranty (one based on the law). Some states prohibit "as is" sales.

Merchantability. An implied warranty of merchantability means that a product must be adequate for its intended purpose.

Fitness. An implied warranty of fitness for a particular purpose means the seller guarantees that the item is fit for a particular purpose—as long as:
- The buyer makes the purpose known;
- The seller knows that the buyer is relying on the seller to provide the proper item or service.

Implied warranties may have time limits governed by state law.

WRITTEN WARRANTIES

On a written warranty, the provider of the warranty must:
- Designate whether the warranty is full or limited on goods that cost more than $10;
- State the coverage in clear, easy-to-read language on one document on goods that cost more than $15;
- Make available the warranty on goods that cost more than $15 so the consumer can read it.

4 Warranty information is usually in the fine print. Read it.

SERVICE CONTRACTS

M*any people wonder whether it's worth buying a service contract. Your decision should include asking who's offering the service, what's covered, and the length of time the item will be expected to function properly.*

THEY'RE NOT WARRANTIES

Service contracts are sometimes called extended warranties but they're not warranties. A warranty comes as part of the item's purchase price. Extended warranties cost extra. However, both provide repair of the item during a specified time frame.

There are three general types of extended warranties and service contracts:

Manufacturer. These are sold and serviced by the manufacturer for their products alone. They're sold directly by the retailer or by the manufacturer, generally for large appliances or electronics.

Dealer/retailer. These are sold directly by the retailer who sets the price and types of service available. You generally have to contact the retailer for service.

Independent. These are "third-party" companies that offer service contracts on many types of products from different manufacturers. They have no association with the original manufacturer or retailer.

PROFITABLE FOR SELLERS

Extended warranties are often very profitable for the stores that sell them. Extended warranties are not generally recommended because products usually don't fail within the first few years. But you may make the decision to buy an extended warranty for peace of mind and because you don't want to bear the risk that the product you purchased will fail. The salesperson usually receives a commission for selling a service contract or extended warranty.

5 Consider buying an "in-home" extended warranty if the item you buy is too heavy to carry in for repairs.

HOW THEY'RE USED ▶

When you buy a major item—a car, computer, or home appliance—you're usually offered a service contract to repair it. Even many small appliances, such as CD players and hand-held devices, may have service contracts. The purpose of these contracts is to cover repairs after the initial warranty period has expired.

HOME WARRANTIES

A home warranty is a service contract that covers home repair or replacement. It has no relation to your homeowners insurance policy. Unlike homeowners insurance, home warranties may be provided by companies that aren't regulated by your state's insurance department.

Home warranties generally cover major items, such as washers, dryers, ovens, refrigerators, duct work, plumbing, electrical, heating, and air-conditioning systems. Other items or systems could be covered for an additional fee.

You can buy your own home warranty but it may be included in the sale of a house to give the homebuyer some comfort in the systems in the house.

VEHICLE EXTENDED WARRANTIES

You can buy vehicle extended warranties (service contracts) from dealers or insurance companies. A policy may be purchased for one year, or for 12,000 miles, and for longer time periods.

Policies are offered with basic coverage all the way to comprehensive (called bumper to bumper). Not all policies cover rental car reimbursement while your car is in the shop. Check the extended warranty for that coverage.

Per component/occurrence. If you have a policy with a deductible "per component," you will pay the deductible for each of the covered part groups. If you have a policy with a deductible "per occurrence," you will pay each visit for repairs. You can purchase an extended warranty with zero deductible but your premium will be higher.

Waiting period. Before the extended warranty goes into effect, you may find you're not covered during a waiting period. Often an extended warranty may not take effect for the first 30 days after purchase.

Key questions. In considering an extended warranty, ask yourself whether you plan on driving the car past the standard manufacturer warranty, how long you plan on keeping the car, and whether you want the protection afforded by an extended warranty?

WARRANTY

Warranty
ends
Oct.23,2001

EXTENDED
WARRANTY

Warranty
begins
Oct.24,2001

FAILING TO PAY

W*hat if you don't or can't pay for the goods or your debts? What can a debt collector do—and will the seller take back the goods?*

SECURED OR UNSECURED DEBT?

The first question is whether your loan is secured or unsecured. Generally, debts for credit cards, medical providers, and small loans are unsecured. This means you haven't granted the creditor the right to take and sell a specific piece of your property in case you don't repay your debt.

On the other hand, in a secured debt, such as car loans, home loans, and many consumer product loans, you have granted the right to take certain property. The specified property is called *collateral*.

The consequences of failing to make payments on a secured debt should be spelled out precisely in your written agreement. Often the agreement will state that you will be in default of the loan and the creditor will have the right to take the property even if:

- You have missed one payment;
- The property has been lost or it has been destroyed;
- You've sold the property; or,
- You let the required insurance lapse.

STATE LAWS VARY

Every state has rules concerning property seizure. If a purchase is secured by personal property, most lenders won't immediately turn to repossession. Remember that the real value to a seller is your loan—s/he wants to be paid with interest. If you have problems making your payments, contact the lender or the seller and try to negotiate a new payment plan. In some states, the seller needs a court order and the local sheriff to pick up property. In other states, those steps may not be necessary.

A state may allow the lender to come on to your property to take a car without your approval and then sell it. You may be entitled to buy it if you pay the total amount owed plus costs. In most states, if the lender has acted according to law, s/he may also sue you to recover any remaining deficiency.

◀ **A SECURED DEBT**
If you fail to make a payment, a creditor can only repossess the item you pledged as collateral.

UNSECURED CREDITOR'S OPTIONS IF YOU DON'T PAY

If you don't make payments on an unsecured item, the creditor may:
- End the business relationship;
- Report your failure to pay to the credit bureau;
- Sue you to recover the debt.

If the creditor sues you and wins a court judgment, your state's exemption laws will protect certain property from seizure to pay off the debt. Check with a lawyer, legal services program, credit counseling agency, or consumer protection agency for information on exempt property in your state. Check federal and state law to see whether your wages can be garnished. Certain federal benefits can't be seized at all.

DEBT COLLECTORS

The Fair Debt Collection Practices Act (FDCPA) is the key federal law that applies to debt collectors for personal, family, and household debts. Car loans, medical debts, and charge account debts are examples.

It applies only to debt collectors working on behalf of another party, such as a collection agency. Bill collectors working directly for a creditor are not covered under this law.

Under the FDCPA, you're entitled to be treated fairly, without harassment, abuse, or deception. Specifically, the law tells debt collectors they must identify themselves to you on the phone and can only contact you between 8 a.m. and 9 p.m.

If you write to tell a debt collector (as defined under the federal law) to stop contacting you, they must stop. If you are contacted again (except to tell you that collection efforts have ended or that you may be sued), you may have a right to sue for violation of the FDCPA.

DEBT COLLECTORS CAN'T:

- Use obscene or profane language;
- Use or threaten violence;
- Claim you owe more money than you do;
- Add unauthorized interest or charges to the original debt (but can charge interest if originally part of the contract or allowed under state law).
- Contact you at work if they know your employer disapproves;
- Lie to you or threaten imprisonment or seizure of your property.

OTHER RIGHTS

T here are many other consumer protections regarding credit and purchasing. Consumers often inquire about these issues.

WAITING FOR MERCHANDISE

When you order merchandise by mail or phone (including fax and computer), the seller must tell you when s/he expects the merchandise to ship. If no timeframe is given, the time is 30 days. The Mail or Telephone Order Merchandise Rule of the Federal Trade Commission (FTC) governs the seller's obligations in these types of purchases.

The FTC rule applies regardless of "how the merchandise is advertised,

6 Credit card companies may help you resolve disputes with merchants.

how the customer pays, or who initiates the contact."

Your options. If the telephone operator quotes a timeframe, then the seller must meet the deadline or get your consent for a delay. The clock begins when the seller receives a properly-completed order.

If the seller won't ever be able to ship the goods, then s/he must promptly cancel the order and refund your money.

If you paid by cash, check, or money order, the seller must refund the correct amount by first class mail within seven working days after cancellation. If you paid by credit card, the seller must credit your account, or notify you within one billing cycle that the account will not be charged.

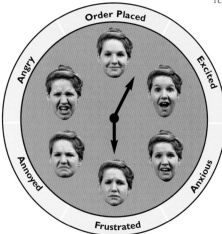

◀ **CONSUMER CONSENT**
If you're told a shipping time frame, you must consent to a delay.

DISCLOSURES ON HOUSEHOLD GOODS

The Consumer Leasing Act (and Regulation M) governs a lease of more than four months for personal, family, or household goods if the total obligation is $25,000 or less. The law does not apply to business leases. Those who lease furniture, cars, musical instruments, appliances, and other goods within the scope of the federal law must provide disclosure before the lease is signed and comply with advertising rules. Before you sign a lease, federal law requires that you receive written information so that you can compare the terms of one lease to another and compare leasing with buying the item. Disclosures include:

- The amount you will pay when you sign the lease;
- The amount of the payments;
- Other charges that you will have to pay;

- The total amount you will pay during the term of the lease;
- Express warranty on the item;
- Default or late payment fees;
- Wear and tear information;
- Whether you can purchase the item at the end of the lease and the cost to purchase it.

Advertising. Federal law and some state laws regulate advertising of consumer leases. An ad must describe the transaction as a lease if certain trigger terms appear in the ad. In addition, it must clearly disclose:

- The total amount of a security deposit or other initial payment;
- The number, amount, due dates, and schedule of periodic payments;
- The purchase terms at lease-end.

Federal law also requires that the advertised lease terms actually be available to you.

STUDENT LOAN DEFAULTS

If your defaulted student loan is assigned to a guaranty agency or the U.S. Department of Education for collection:

- Credit bureaus may be notified and your credit rating may suffer;
- The U.S. Treasury may withhold refund payments toward repayment of your loan;
- There may be collection costs;
- Your wages may be garnished, with your employer sending 10% to 15% of your disposable pay toward your balance;

- Federal employees may have 15% of their disposable pay offset through the Federal Employee Salary Offset Program;
- The Department of Education may sue you for repayment.

Once in default, you're no longer entitled to any deferments or forbearances and may not receive any additional Title IV Federal student aid (if you're in default on any Title IV student loan).

CREDIT DISCRIMINATION

W*hen you apply for credit, the creditor can consider your creditworthiness but can't consider certain personal characteristics.*

BASIC RULES

The Equal Credit Opportunity Act applies to companies that regularly extend credit and requires that you be treated fairly and impartially. Relevant companies include banks, small loan and finance companies, retail and department stores, credit card companies, and credit unions.

When considering whether to offer you a loan, creditors should primarily evaluate whether you have the ability to repay the debt, whether you will repay the debt, and whether the creditor has protection if you don't pay.

APPROPRIATE CONSIDERATIONS

The following questions are appropriate to this evaluation:

- What is your occupation? Length of employment? Salary?
- What are your expenses? Number of dependents? Obligations, such as alimony or child support?
- What is your credit record? How much debt is outstanding?
- How long have you lived at your address? Do you own or rent?
- Do you have other resources, such as savings?

Immigration status is an appropriate consideration.

HOUSING LOANS

The Equal Credit Opportunity Act also applies to mortgage and home-improvement loans. In addition to prohibiting discrimination against you based on your personal characteristics, the law also prohibits discrimination based on the race or national origin of the neighborhood.

Creditors are prohibited from using an appraisal that includes consideration of race in the neighborhood. You may request a copy of the appraisal that you paid for and it must be provided to you.

7 If you believe you've been unfairly denied credit, contact the federal agency identified in the creditor's rejection notice.

NOTICE

Federal law requires that creditors notify you within 30 days whether your loan has been approved or denied. If you are denied credit, the notice must be in writing and the specific reasons must be provided.

PROHIBITED CONSIDERATIONS

Federal law prohibits denial of credit based on race, sex, marital status, religion, age, national origin, or receipt of public income (veterans' benefits, welfare, and social security). If you exercise your rights in good faith under federal consumer credit laws, a lender also can't use that fact to discriminate against you. Discrimination includes:

- Discouraging you from applying for a loan;
- Denying you a loan as long as you otherwise qualify for the loan;
- Giving you different terms than other people with a history similar to yours;
- Closing an account.

Some prohibited factors may be considered in certain ways that bear on creditworthiness. For example, the lender can consider how long until you retire. The lender can also consider whether you will continue to be eligible for public benefits.

DIFFERENT DECISIONS

Creditors may reach different lending decisions because they have different risk thresholds.

DISCRIMINATION AGAINST WOMEN

The law protects both men and women from discrimination but the law was intended to address certain problems creditors had often used to deny credit to women.

Marital status. Whether you are married, single, widowed, divorced, or separated, your marital status cannot be used to deny you credit.

Wrong questions. To ensure that women have protection, creditors:

- Can't generally ask your gender on an application form, except for a loan to buy or build a home, and you don't have to check off a title (Miss, Mrs., or Ms.);
- Can't ask about childbearing plans or birth control;
- Can't consider whether you have a telephone listing in your name (but you may be asked if you have a telephone);
- Must consider all your income, even if it's child support, alimony, or part-time employment;
- Must allow you a credit account in your own name if you're otherwise creditworthy.

◀ YOU'VE GOT THE POWER
Women have protection under anti-discrimination laws.

21

INVESTING RIGHTS

The cornerstones of investing rights are the disclosure of information to help investors make informed decisions and the regulation of securities professionals.

SECURITIES

Securities are required to be registered with the Securities and Exchange Commission (SEC) to keep investors informed about the financial status of the securities issuer. You can find information about:

● The issuer's property and business;
● The security being offered;
● The management;
● The financial status of the company.

Registration statements are available to the public and on the Internet through the SEC's EDGAR database.

WHO'S WATCHING?

To achieve its oversight mission, the SEC relies in part on private, member-owned and member-operated securities industry organizations, known as self-regulatory organizations (SROs). The New York Stock Exchange (NYSE) and the National Association of Securities Dealers (NASD) are examples of SROs. SROs regulate their members and have responsibilities under the federal securities laws.

IT'S A FACT

Private securities offerings don't need to be registered if they're limited to a number of persons or institutions; of a limited size; intrastate offerings; or federal, state, and local government securities.

GET THE FACTS

Ask and get answers to three simple questions before investing your money:

● Is the investment registered? Some types of small companies are not required to register with the SEC, but your state securities regulator will have information about any legitimate company issuing stock.
● Is the seller of the investment licensed? Firms and individuals selling investments should be licensed for business in your state. The NASD has this information as does your state securities regulatory agency.
● Does the investment sound too good to be true? Don't believe in "guaranteed" or "risk-free" returns, or claims of astronomical returns over a short period of time. If anyone makes these claims, they're committing a crime.

THE SEC PROTECTS INVESTORS

The SEC protects investors by investigating:

- Insider trading (which means that a person who has a relationship of trust and confidence has bought or sold a security based on material, non-public information);
- Misrepresentation or omission of material information;
- Manipulating stock prices;
- Theft of customer's funds;
- Violations of the broker-dealer's obligation to treat customers fairly;
- Selling securities that were not properly registered.

THINGS TO KNOW

- The SEC does not regulate a timeframe in which a trade must be executed. But, if a firm does advertise their timeframe, the firm can't exaggerate and must inform investors that there could be significant delays.

- If you open an account, the brokerage firm may ask you to sign a contract that requires arbitration of disputes. If you sign this provision, you will be waiving your right to sue if there's a dispute and relying on arbitration to settle the dispute.

- You can obtain annual and other reports from the SEC for those companies with more than $10 million in assets and more than 500 shareholders.

BROKER/DEALERS

Broker/dealers must register with the SEC, an exchange, or the NASD, and generally with their state securities agency. People associated with broker/dealers may be required to register with their state securities agency. To find information about the records of broker/dealers, you can contact the NASD's "Public Disclosure Program." Through this program, you can find out whether the person has been disciplined or had a criminal conviction.

INVESTMENT ADVISORS

Each state has regulatory authority over investment advisor firms with less than $25 million in assets under management, while the SEC regulates those with $25 million or more. Approximately 19,000 of the 25,000 investment advisors and financial planners across the nation fall under state authority. Before considering assistance from investment advisors, check your state securities agency or the SEC to see whether they're properly registered.

COMPLAINTS

What can you do if you have a complaint about a broker or advisor?

- Talk to your broker or advisor;
- Talk to the branch manager;
- Write to the compliance department of your firm's main office;
- Contact the SEC or nearest office of NASD Regulation, if applicable;
- Contact your state securities agency.

PRIVACY RIGHTS

You may have the right to say "It's none of your business!" How well can you protect your privacy today?

YOUR CREDIT HISTORY

It takes your vigilance to be sure that credit bureaus do not report incorrect or outdated information to retailers, banks, landlords, mortgage companies, or the government.

WHAT INFORMATION IS IN A REPORT?

Your credit history report includes your name, current and prior addresses, current and prior employment, Social Security number, credit accounts and payment history, public record information (for example, lawsuits, bankruptcy), and who has received a copy of your report.

Banks and stores report information to credit bureaus. A creditor will typically check your credit history record using one of three national credit bureaus when you apply for a loan, credit card, utility, etc.

DO I PAY FOR A REPORT?

Depending on the state where you live, each credit bureau can charge you for your credit report, usually about $8.50. There is no charge for a report within 60 days of being denied credit, insurance, or employment, based on information in the report. If you are on welfare, are unemployed and plan to look for a job, or if your report is inaccurate because you are a victim of fraud, you are entitled to one free report annually.

YOUR RIGHTS

In regard to your credit report, you have the right to:

- Add an explanation to your credit report if the dispute is unresolved;
- Know who checked your credit record in the last year (for most purposes) and in the last two years for employment purposes;
- Know which credit bureau was contacted if you apply for and are denied credit based on your report.

8 Non-profit organizations are available in most states to help consumers with debt issues.

THE FAIR CREDIT REPORTING ACT

The Fair Credit Reporting Act addresses who can obtain credit history reports, how long adverse information can appear on the report, procedures for consumer consent to obtain a report for employment purposes, the procedures if the consumer disputes the accuracy of the report, and penalties for violation of the act.

Those who supply information (including banks and stores) to credit bureaus have certain obligations to avoid and correct errors. Consumers can provide information to credit bureaus that must be weighed against those who initially furnished the entry. The credit bureau and the furnisher of the information must investigate disputed information. Credit bureaus must delete information that cannot be verified.

YOUR CREDIT REPORT

Monitor your credit reports once or twice a year. If you find an error or incomplete information, contact the three major credit bureaus and the party who furnished the disputed item.

Call this number with questions -
Request Reference:
Report Date: 12 November 1999

CREDIT PROFILE

Personal Identification Information
Mary Smith
55 Main St.
Town, State 99999

Social Security Number:
Date of Birth:

Credit Account Information

Company Name		Account Number and Whose Account	Date Opened	Last Activity	Type of Account and Status	High Credit	Terms	Items as of Date Reported Balance	Past Due	Date Reported
Nationwide Mortgage	Individual Account									
Real estate mortgage Conventional mortgage			05/99	10/99	Installment Pays as agreed	$371K	$1935	$369K		10/99
Express	Individual Account									
Credit card			06/86	07/99	Open Pays as agreed	$0			$0	10/99
VISA	Individual Account		10/84	09/99	Revolving Pays as agreed			$0		10/99
state mortgage	Joint Account		04/93	04/99	Installment Pays as agreed	$410K	$2866	$1994 $0		09/99
	Individual Account		03/95	05/95	Revolving Pays as agreed	$1000		$0		05/99
			05/99	07/99	Revolving	$12000		$0		09/99

TELEPHONE, MAIL, AND E-MAIL PROMOTIONS

You can choose to say "no" to phone and other types of solicitations.

TELEMARKETERS

The Telephone Consumer Protection Act addresses unsolicited telemarketing calls, automated and pre-recorded phone calls, and faxes.

Under the Federal Communications Commission's telemarketing rules, you have the right to certain information:

- The name of the caller and the party on whose behalf s/he is calling;
- A phone number or address at which that party may be contacted;
- The identity of the party using an artificial (computerized) voice or prerecorded voice message and a phone number or address during or after the message.

CREDIT CARD OFFERS

Watch out for the infamous "you're pre-approved" letters. These are computer-produced with personal information from advertising and credit bureaus. To remove your name from their lists, you can call this toll-free number: 888-5-OPTOUT (888-567-8688) for all three credit bureaus.

OTHER FEDERAL LAWS AND RULES

Federal provisions help protect consumers from being lured into a scam. For example, telemarketers must tell consumers:

- The odds of winning a prize or the factors used to calculate odds;
- That you don't have to pay a fee or buy something to win a prize or participate in a promotion;
- What you will have to pay or the conditions you will have to meet to receive or redeem a prize.

The Deceptive Mail Prevention and Enforcement Act protects consumers from fraudulent sweepstakes promotions by mail. The law prohibits:

- Claims that you're a winner if you aren't one;
- A purchase to enter the contest;
- Mailing simulated checks that fail to state clearly that they aren't actually checks;
- Any symbols or words that imply the federal government is associated with the sweepstakes.

DON'T CALL ME

To stop telemarketing calls and mail promotions, you must tell the caller or sender to remove your name from the list. To reduce (but not eliminate) contacts from national lists, you need to inform the Direct Marketing Association (DMA). You will need to identify yourself and request to be removed from marketing lists. Here's the contact information:

E-mail. Direct Marketing Association, E-mail Preference Service: www.e-mps.org;

Mail. Direct Marketing Association, Mail Preference Service, P.O. Box 9008, Farmingdale, N.Y. 11735-9008.

Telephone. Direct Marketing Association, Telephone Preference Service, P.O. Box 9014, Farmingdale, N.Y. 11735-9014. Even after you've registered, you will still have to tell new callers that you want to be removed from the caller's list.

9 Telemarketing calls are only allowed between 8 a.m. and 9 p.m. (your local time).

WHICH IS WHICH?

- A sweepstakes awards prizes or items of value based on chance and there's no entry fee to win.
- A lottery awards items of value by chance to those who pay to participate. Lotteries are illegal unless they're state-operated or fall under an exempt category (for example, a charity).
- A skill contest awards items of value by skill (not chance). There may be an entry fee, purchase, or donation to participate.

PERSONAL AND FINANCIAL IDENTITY

Victims of burglaries report that they feel "violated" by the entry into their homes. If your identity is taken, the feeling can be quite the same. In 1998, Congress passed a law making identity theft a federal crime.

STEALING IDENTITIES

Thieves get your records by:

- Intercepting pre-approved credit card offers from the mail or picking your discarded, cancelled, and unused checks, credit card receipts, or bank statements from your trash;
- "Shoulder-surfing" at the ATM locations to get your PIN (Personal Identification Number) or simply walking into the bank and pretending to be you;
- Calling and pretending to be a bank or government official, or a merchant confirming your account numbers;
- Calling to say that you've won a prize that you can collect for a small delivery fee if you provide your account information;
- Bribing employees of stores or credit companies to get different types of information about you.

Often people don't know they're victims until months after the thief has stolen their documents and used their identity. Victims typically learn about identity theft when bills arrive or they receive calls from bill collectors.

WHAT TO DO

If you receive letters, calls, or bills demanding payment for things you didn't order, act quickly.

- Report the crime to the police. You may have to visit the local station to fill out a crime report.
- Contact the three national credit bureaus (Experian, Trans Union Corporation, and Equifax Credit Information Services) so that it won't appear on your credit report.
- Call and follow-up with a letter to credit card companies and request they immediately close all your accounts. When you request the closing of the account, have the credit card company mark "closed at customer request."
- Cancel all your checking and saving accounts and request all new account numbers and PIN's. Place a *stop payment* on all outstanding checks and call the people to explain the situation. Send them replacement checks right away.

IT'S A CRIME

Under the Identity Theft and Assumption Deterrence Act, it's a federal crime to "knowingly transfer or use, without lawful authority, a means of identification of another" with the intent to commit "any unlawful activity" that is a felony under federal or state/local law. A "means of identification" includes a name, Social Security number, credit card number, cellular telephone serial number, or other item that can identify a specific individual. More than 35 states have specific laws relating to identity theft. In the states without specific laws against identity theft, the laws may prohibit the activity under other provisions.

PREVENTING IDENTITY THEFT

Being observant of your financial surroundings can help you avoid identity theft. Here are some ways you can minimize the risk of identity theft:

- Empty your wallet of unneeded credit cards, and other identification;
- Keep a list in a safe place of all cards in your wallet, including membership cards, account numbers, customer service numbers, and names of family members on the accounts;
- Never write your credit card number or Social Security number on a check. If a merchant won't accept your check without this information, take your business elsewhere. There are online services for merchants to verify and guarantee the check;

- Don't write your PIN's or passwords on your credit cards. Avoid using the last four digits of your Social Security number, your birth date, your spouse's name, or any easily recognized words as a PIN;
- Install a locked mailbox at your home;
- Notify your credit card company or bank if you don't receive your statement on the usual date of the month;
- Tear up or shred unsolicited credit offers, cancelled checks, statements, and credit card receipts;
- Don't give out personal or financial information over the phone unless you called the party.

SECURING PRIVACY ONLINE

I magine someone following you from store to store noting your every move, looking over your shoulder as you skim the newspaper, or recording your TV channel decisions to see what shows and ads you watched.

YOUR PRIVACY

Technology on the Internet has made possible a shadow patrol over your visiting practices. A website can tell what kind of computer and software you are using, where you are accessing from, and other websites you have just visited.

When you visit a website, it may ask for information about you. It can tie this information with your browsing habits to build a "profile" of you, which can be sold to other companies. If you are asked for a password to access the website, use a different password on different websites and, of course, don't tell anyone your password.

WHERE'S THE POLICY?

There's usually a link to the policy on the first page of a website. If the company doesn't post a policy, e-mail them and ask them to post it online. This should be a statement on how the company collects information and what they do with it. The website should tell you whether it discloses information to a third party.

BE WARY

It's a federal crime to intercept e-mails in transmission. Your Internet provider can look at your messages but not disclose the messages—with certain exceptions. Your provider may also have an End-User Agreement, that you signed, explaining what it can do with e-mails.

The e-commerce industry has developed third-party review programs that evaluate websites and award certification if the website meets specific criteria. BBBOnline (a subsidiary of the Better Business Bureaus) and TRUSTe seals are two examples of seal programs. With the seal, e-consumers should expect that the website has met the guidelines for protecting privacy. Consumers can complain to these programs if the site fails to comply with privacy policies.

At this stage of the Internet's evolution, you should ask who, what, when, where, and why, if someone requests personal information on the Internet. As long as government and the Internet industry don't have a comprehensive privacy program, consumers will have to be wary about disclosing their personal information online.

KIDS' PRIVACY

Children's online privacy is protected by the Children Online Privacy Protection Act of 1998. The federal law now places certain requirements on web operators.

When entering a website directed toward children under 13-years of age, look for a privacy policy that details the company's rules on data collection and information on:

- Kinds of information being collected and what is being disclosed;
- Parental permission to collect information;
- Parental permission to give information to third parties;
- Revoking parental permission at any time;
- Parental review of information your child has provided;
- Parental requests to delete any information previously collected and future emails to your child.

The Child Online Protection Act protects kids online under age 17 from the dissemination of objectionable materials that are defined in the law as "harmful to minors." This law was immediately challenged on First Amendment grounds.

Parents need to emphasize responsible use of the Internet and use access controls they can set to monitor and protect children from objectionable or offensive material online.

IS THE WEBSITE SECURE?

Don't complete online forms that ask for personal information, such as credit card accounts, unless the website is secure. On most web browsers, there's a "key" that appears on the screen indicating that the website has encoding software so that only the host computer can read the information. If your browser can't tell if a website is secure, don't give out personal or financial information.

31

Other Privacy Issues

Privacy of medical records is currently the subject of considerable debate. This issue and others are raised frequently as concerns for consumers.

Medical Records

Privacy advocates, legislators, insurance companies, employers and others are considering the privacy of medical records. The debate is at both the federal and state levels. A few states have adopted a medical records privacy act.

In addition to your medical providers, your medical records are generally available to your HMO or insurance carrier. You may have also signed waivers that allowed information to be shared with others in applying for insurance coverage or when you visited a provider.

Approximately half of the states give patients a statutory right to see and copy their own medical records. Even if you live in a state that has not expressly provided that right to you, you may still be able to have access to your medical records.

You should first check whether your doctor or hospital has a procedure to obtain medical records. Expect that your local doctor or hospital will require a written request for a copy of the records. A hospital may ask for a patient number and admission date. They may have a special form to be completed. Depending on your state rules, the hospital or doctor may charge for the cost of labor and copying of the records.

If the doctor or hospital does not cooperate with your request, you should call the local medical society or state insurance office to find out your rights to the records. If you are within your state's rights, you may need a letter from an attorney to get your records.

HEALTH AND LONGEVITY DATABASE

If you apply for insurance, you must give your consent before the insurance company can obtain a consumer report, such as a report from the Medical Information Bureau (MIB). MIB is an association of 600 life insurance companies whose database contains health and longevity condition information on millions of Americans and Canadians. When conditions and findings are significant to the health and longevity of the applicant, the insurance company submits the applicant's coded information to MIB. Approximately 15 of 100 applicants for individual life, health, or disability insurance are submitted to MIB.

MIB has no claims data and no medical records. It purges information after seven years (under the Fair Credit Reporting Act).

If MIB has a record on you, you probably will have to pay a processing fee to obtain a copy of the information.

Contact MIB at P.O. Box 105, Essex Station, Boston, MA, 02112; 617-426-3660; www.mib.com.

DO YOU AGREE TO SHARE?

When you're at a doctor's office or in the hospital, you may be asked to sign a release. The release gives the provider your authorization or consent to share your medical records. Before signing the release, examine the authorization to be sure you know, understand, and agree with who may receive a copy of your medical records.

TENANT'S RIGHTS TO PRIVACY

Tenants often worry about their landlord entering their rental units. As a general rule, landlords cannot just enter the rental unit to check up on the tenant. A landlord can usually enter the rental unit if:

- There is an emergency;
- You give permission;
- The landlord has provided advance notice.

Some state laws specify notice of one or two days.

 10 A video store can't disclose your personal information (including tape selections) except in limited circumstances.

PERSONAL INFORMATION

Several states do not permit merchants to record personal information when a consumer uses a credit card. Visa and MasterCard also prohibit merchants from requiring a customer's telephone number when the customer uses their cards.

YOUR HOUSING RIGHTS

You're entitled to certain disclosures before purchasing a house and laws protect you against discrimination. In rental housing, both landlord and tenant have responsibilities.

PURCHASING A HOME

The process of buying a home includes several points at which buyers are entitled to specific information.

PROPER NOTICE

The Real Estate Settlement Procedures Act (RESPA) requires that homebuyers receive disclosures of information at various points in the home buying process. For example, when you apply for a loan, the lender must give you a Good Faith Estimate of the settlement service charges within three business days. RESPA also requires that:

- The lender tell you in writing within three business days whether it expects another firm to service your loan;

 File a fair housing complaint with the US Department of Housing and Urban Development or the appropriate state agency.

- The lender disclose its "affiliates" so you know what the relationship is between the lender and the party to which the lender referred you;
- The homebuyer get the HUD-1 Settlement Sheet one business day before settlement. It lists the services provided and charged to you.

If your lender requires you to have an escrow account, RESPA limits the amount to a maximum of two months' payments.

DISCRIMINATION

Federal law prohibits housing discrimination based on race, color, national origin, religion, sex, family status, or disability. Some state and local laws may address housing discrimination and provide protections for other groups.

Under the Fair Housing Act, new multifamily houses with four or more units must be designed and built to allow access to a disabled person.

- Federal law gives consumers the right to know the terms, rates, and conditions for home equity lines of credit at the time of their application and before the first transaction. Lenders are restricted in making changes after the home equity plan has been opened.

- Home sellers may be obligated by state law to disclose problems that impact on the property's value and make certain written disclosures to the buyer. In most states, fraudulently concealing a physical defect from the buyer is illegal.

▼ ESCROW ACCOUNTS
Lenders may require buyers to put taxes and insurance premiums into an account so the lender can ensure payment.

PRIVATE MORTGAGE INSURANCE

Homeowners have certain rights regarding cancellation of Private Mortgage Insurance (PMI). With certain exceptions, if you're current on your payments, lenders must automatically terminate PMI when you reach 22 percent equity or you can request cancellation of PMI when you reach 20 percent equity in your residence.

HOMEOWNER'S INSURANCE

As a homeowner, you will probably get insurance to protect your home and belongings.

HOMEOWNER'S INSURANCE

Lenders require homeowner's insurance to protect their financial interest in your property. This insurance (usually called hazard insurance) generally covers the home against fire, smoke, wind, hail, vandalism, or other similar acts. If the house is destroyed by a covered event, the insurance company will often pay the lender directly.

In addition to what the lender requires for insurance coverage, you will generally also have comprehensive homeowner's coverage which covers your personal belongings for damage or loss.

For particularly expensive items, you may want to consider adding specific coverage. A homeowner or renter's policy may include liability coverage. Liability coverage insures you if, for example, a guest slips and falls in your home or another accident occurs.

> **12** Renter's insurance does not cover loss to the building or land, but covers a renter's personal property.

DOG BITE COVERAGE

The liability coverage for a dog bite should be a special concern if you own a dog—or a breed—known for dangerous tendencies. Be sure your insurance company is aware of your dog's breed and any biting incidents.

NATIONAL FLOOD INSURANCE ACT

Homeowner's policies don't cover flood losses. Flood insurance must be bought separately and is available only in communities that participate in the National Flood Insurance Program (NFIP).

There's usually a 30-day waiting period before the policy becomes effective unless:

- The policy is bought in connection with purchasing, renewing, increasing, or extending a mortgage or construction loan; or,
- The policy is bought during the 13-month period after a change to a flood insurance rate map.

Under federal law, a lender must tell you whether the home is in a flood hazard area.

BE PREPARED BEFORE A LOSS

Create and update a written, picture, or video inventory of your personal items as follows:

- Go from room to room and open all drawers, closets, and cabinets;
- Be sure to detail all small items, perhaps include a photo of the item with a measuring ruler to show size;
- For larger items, note or focus on the model and serial numbers of the item;
- Don't forget the garage, storage areas, outside furniture, and built-ins;
- Make a new inventory every two years or whenever you acquire a major item.

Be sure to store your inventory in a safe place.

AFTER A LOSS

If you've suffered a loss to your home or furnishings, immediately take steps to secure your property. Board up windows and doors to prevent further loss, move your personal items to a safe area, and cover holes in your roof. When you've safely secured your property, call your agent or insurance company to report the loss. Have the following information available to give to the agent:

- Type of loss and any official (police, fire department) reports;
- List of property lost or damaged (use your inventory including videos, photos, written lists);
- Any costs (with receipts) you have incurred to further protect your property;
- Temporary housing or food needs for your family.

IT'S A FACT

As of April 2000, the average annual cost of a flood insurance policy was $353 and the average amount of flood insurance purchased was $124,089.

◀ REPLACEMENT OR MARKET VALUE

Most experts recommend that homeowners insure their homes and contents for replacement value with inflation adjustments.

RENTAL HOUSING

Rental housing can include an apartment, condo, single-family house, trailer, or even a piece of land where you pitch a tent. Under the agreement, each party has obligations to the other.

ORAL AGREEMENTS

An oral agreement is legal as long as it covers a period of one year or less. The landlord agrees to let you move in and you agree to pay a certain amount on a regular schedule. Because misunderstandings can easily occur in oral agreements, parties generally prefer a written document.

WRITTEN AGREEMENTS

These agreements may be for a short period of time and automatically renewed at the end of the period. An example may be an agreement for a month-to-month rental. In these situations, you can move out with proper notice, usually 30 days, and not owe any more rent.

SECURITY DEPOSITS

Landlords can collect security deposits when you move in. The purpose is to ensure payment of the rent and the general condition of the rental unit. State law may limit the amount that a landlord can charge. In those states, the limit will typically be a month or two rent. Landlords may also be required to keep the security deposit in a separate account in order to make sure it's available when you leave. They may also be required to return the deposit within a specific number of days (generally within 30 days after you leave).

Landlords have the right to withhold part of the security deposit for repairs beyond normal wear and tear, although the landlord may have to provide an itemized list of deductions from the security deposit. You have the right to sue the landlord for the security deposit if s/he fails to comply with state law or the terms of the lease.

LEASES

These are written agreements, often on preprinted forms, that spell out the details of the lease. A lease is for a definite time period, usually one to three years.

Preprinted leases are usually written in favor of the landlord, but you have the right to ask for changes. If you disagree with the terms of a provision, ask for it to be changed. Any change must by initialed and dated by the landlord (or agent) and the renter.

Both tenant and landlord are bound by the terms as long as either party does not break the lease. For example:

- If you don't pay rent according to the lease schedule, the landlord can end the lease and evict you as long as the state laws are followed for eviction;
- Generally, if the landlord does not provide the agreed-upon services, such as hot water, repairs, or trash collection, you can leave the property.

Unless the landlord has broken the terms of the lease, you must continue to pay rent. In a few states, the law may protect the tenant who needs to break the lease for special reasons, such as health or job relocation, and release the tenant from further rent.

13 If you stay past the term of your lease, the law will generally consider you to have become a month-to-month tenant.

REPAIRS

Landlords are generally required under state and local laws to maintain rental units so they're habitable. A habitable rental unit is one that has adequate heat, water, weatherproofing, electricity, and is sanitary. Building and housing codes may specify the standards that must be met. If your landlord fails to meet these responsibilities, you may have several options. Because laws vary from state to state, you should check the law before exercising these options:

- Pay partial rent;
- Withhold rent;
- Make repairs and deduct them from the rent;
- Contact your local building inspector; and/or,
- Move out from the rental unit.

RENTER'S INSURANCE

A tenant's loss of personal belongings from a fire or theft is not covered by a landlord's insurance policy. To be covered for these types of losses and personal liability, a renter needs a renter's insurance policy. Expect the policy to have a deductible that affects your premium and that you will pay in the event of a loss before the policy will pay.

RENTAL ASSISTANCE PROGRAMS

T*he federal government funds several programs that provide rental assistance to those in need.*

TYPES OF PROGRAMS

Public housing. Public housing provides rental housing for eligible low-income families, the elderly, and persons with disabilities in a variety of structures, from scattered single family homes to high-rise apartments. A local housing agency, usually a city or county agency, operates public housing and handles applications.

If you apply for public housing, are eligible, and are offered a spot, you will have to sign a lease that may include a security deposit. Rent is determined by a family's gross annual income less deductions, if any.

Vouchers. Section 8 rental vouchers and rental certificate program provide rental assistance that allows an eligible person to use the voucher to cover all or part of the rent. In this program, participants find their own places to rent from privately-owned housing, which may include single-family homes, townhouses, and apartments. The participant isn't restricted to units in subsidized housing projects but can choose any housing that meets the program's requirements for health and safety. The local housing agency administers the vouchers and rental certificates.

Subsidized housing. Privately-owned subsidized housing gives property owners direct subsidies and the owner applies the subsidies to the rents charged to low-income tenants.

HUD's RESIDENTS' RESPONSIBILITIES

Residents have a responsibility to do the following:

● Comply with the terms of the lease;

● Pay rent on time each month;

● Provide accurate information for rental eligibility determinations and consent to verify the information;

● Don't disturb neighbors;

● Not engage in criminal activity;

● Keep the unit and the common areas or grounds clean;

● Properly dispose of garbage and waste;

● Comply with local health and safety codes;

● Maintain the condition of your unit and common areas;

● Report maintenance problems in your unit or common areas to the management.

IT'S A FACT

Approximately 3,300 housing agencies administer public housing for approximately 1.3 million American households.

Source: U.S. Department of Housing and Urban Development

HUD'S RESIDENTS' RIGHTS

Residents have the right to:

- Decent, safe, and sanitary housing;
- Timely repairs;
- Prior notice before entry into an apartment when it is not an emergency;
- Organize without hindrance from the property owners or management;
- Post materials about tenants' rights;
- Use the common areas for tenants to gather to consider the issues regarding the property;
- Have input into residential community affairs;
- Not to be subject to discrimination based on race, color, religion, gender, disability, family status, national origin, or age.

If any of these rights are taken away and you have maintained your part of the lease, you should consider taking these actions:

- Talk to the landlord or agent first who may be unaware of the problem and want to resolve it quickly. Give the landlord adequate time to solve the problem. A broken hot-water heater should be repaired in 24 hours but resurfacing the parking lot will take longer;
- If the situation is life-threatening or creating a public nuisance, then you might have to call your city health or building department. If it's appropriate, inspectors will follow-up on your complaint;
- If the landlord refuses to make the repair, you might be able to make these repairs or have them made by a third party and deduct the cost of the repairs from your next rent payment. You should contact your local housing agency, state consumer agency, or legal aid office to determine if your state laws permit this action.

INSURANCE RIGHTS

Insurance policies contain the terms of the contract with the policyholder but the consumer does not typically read the policy cover-to-cover until a loss occurs or a claim needs to be made.

LIFE INSURANCE

An individual should consider having 6-8 times their annual salary in life insurance. This is a general rule and will vary according to budget, family size, spouse's ability to work, other life insurance sources, and outside income.

IT'S A FACT

There are more than 2,000 life insurance companies (and more financial institutions) in the United States that sell life insurance.

RIGHTS REGARDING INSURANCE DENIALS

Insurance companies who use consumer reports to deny insurance, increase rates, or terminate a policy, must comply with the Fair Credit Reporting Act.

Insurance companies must notify you that they plan to check with an agency supplying consumer reports and receive your consent.

If the company makes an adverse decision (denial or increased premiums, for example), it must:

- Tell you the source of the consumer report and provide information on how to contact the company;
- Give you notice that you have a right to challenge the accuracy or completeness of the information that it received and that you have a right to a free consumer report from the company within 60 days.

DECEPTIVE PRACTICES

Churning. If you have a whole life policy and it has built up considerable cash value, an insurance agent may persuade you to purchase a so-called better, new, or improved policy. If you cash in the value of your policy for the new one, the agent will make a commission and you will no longer have the cash value of the old policy. You will have to start over to build cash value. This practice is called churning and is illegal.

Vanishing premiums. Another deceptive practice is an agent promising you that after a period, you won't have to pay premiums because the company's investment will cover them. Predictions of *vanishing premiums* then don't turn out to be accurate and the company requires you to pay the premiums. Since no one can predict investment returns, be wary of promises that premiums won't have to be paid in the future.

COMPANY RATINGS

When you buy life insurance, you don't expect to collect the death benefit payout for years (or decades) in the future. For this reason, it is important to evaluate the company that wants to sell you insurance. Standard & Poor's and Duff & Phelps provide company ratings, which you can find at various sources on the Internet or by asking an insurance company.

THINGS TO KNOW

- If you have a policy with cash value when you die, your beneficiaries will get only the death benefit—not the death benefit and the cash value of the policy.

- Most companies offer a 30-day grace period to pay the premium. If you can't pay, the policy will lapse. Sometimes you can pay whole life policy premiums through the cash value. If you can't pay because you become disabled and you signed a "waiver of premium" provision, you don't have to pay while disabled.

- To be approved for all types of life insurance policies, you will have to satisfy certain medical criteria. Depending on your age, health, and the policy you want, you may have to take a medical exam. Generally if you're part of a group policy from work, you don't have to take an exam.

▼ ARE THERE HOLES IN YOUR UMBRELLA?
You will know if you read your policy and ask questions.

43

HEALTH INSURANCE

Federal law generally provides protections when you leave a job or take an unpaid leave for family and medical reasons.

GENERAL RULES

Generally, state and federal laws don't require employers to provide health insurance. If the employer does provide insurance, then certain federal and state laws may apply The employer may need to have a minimum number of employees before the law applies.

MEDICARE AND MEDICAID

Medicare is the federal program that provides hospital and medical coverage to those who are 65 years or older and qualified for Social Security. Medical coverage generally requires monthly premium payments.

Medicaid is the state program that provides coverage to low-income individuals and certain other needy groups. The eligibility requirements for each state vary.

WHO HAS INSURANCE?

About 70% of the population has health insurance coverage. More than 60% have employment-based health insurance.

FAMILY AND MEDICAL LEAVE ACT

Federal law requires employers (federal, state, and local governments, and private employers with 50 or more employees) to give employees up to 12 work weeks of unpaid leave a year with protection for their job and continued group health benefits during the leave. Reasons for leave include:

- Birth and care of a newborn or placement and care of adopted children.
- Care for the employee or an immediate family member with a serious health problem.

WHO REGULATES HEALTHCARE COVERAGE?

If an insurance company is providing health coverage, then your state insurance commission regulates that company. If the health plan is self-funded by a private-sector employer or union, you may complain to the U.S. Department of Labor (DOL) Pension and Welfare Benefits Administration. Although the DOL does not interpret provisions of any particular health benefit plan or require employers to pay claims, it may investigate your complaint.

RIGHTS WHEN LEAVING A JOB

When you resign from a job (with certain exceptions), your job is eliminated, you divorce, or the employee covering you dies, you're entitled to an extension of your prior health coverage under COBRA (Consolidated Omnibus Budget Reconciliation Act).

COBRA is not free insurance. You must pay for it, but you will be able to get the group insurance rates you had when you were employed. You will now pay the portion your employer previously paid for you. You, your employer, and the plan all have obligations in order to trigger the law:

- Your employer must inform the plan of your status;
- Your plan must notify you of your COBRA rights;
- You must notify the plan of changes in family status;
- You must decide within 60 days of the end of the employer-paid coverage whether you want to continue the coverage.

The Health Insurance Portability and Accountability Act protects people who leave their jobs and have serious medical conditions. Under this law, if there has been no lapse in the coverage of 63 days or more, you won't have the usual pre-existing condition exclusions. Employees with chronic conditions can't be charged a higher premium than other employees. Furthermore, employees who have a baby can enroll the child in their insurance plan immediately, rather than waiting for the next open enrollment period.

▼ **COBRA RIGHTS**
The extension of insurance coverage under your previous employer's plan may be from 18 to 36 months.

IT'S A FACT

Medicare, the nation's largest health insurance program, provides coverage for 39 million Americans. The program covers approximately 13% of the population.

AUTOMOBILE RIGHTS

To protect consumer purchases and automobile
leases, state and federal governments
have adopted numerous measures.

LEASING A VEHICLE

When leasing, you're paying for the use of the vehicle plus normal wear and tear. Making lease payments may cost you less than paying finance charges. At the end of the lease, however, you don't own or have equity in the vehicle. To understand leasing, you need first to understand its language.

UP-FRONT COSTS

Lease inception fees usually include the first month's payment, a refundable security deposit, a down payment (called *capitalized cost reduction*), taxes, registration, and other fees.

MONTHLY PAYMENTS

Monthly payments for a lease vehicle are usually lower than payments for purchasing the vehicle. With a lease, you pay for the vehicle's depreciation plus the use charges (just like renting vehicle). In addition, taxes and fees are added to your payment each month.

ENDING THE LEASE EARLY

You should know what the charges will be if you decide to return the vehicle early. Many leases impose early termination and default penalty clause to compensate the leasing company for the lost payments and the cost of releasing or disposing of the vehicle.

CLOSED-END AND OPEN-END LEASES

At the end of a *closed-end* lease, you walk away after you pay the end-of-lease charges, such as excess mileage and wear and tear. With an *open-end* lease, your payment, when you turn the car in at the end of the lease, is the difference between the original contract value and the lessor's appraised value at the end of the lease.

EXCESS MILEAGE AND EXCESS WEAR

Most leases generally limit you to 12,000-15,000 miles per year. If you exceed the mileage limit, you will have to pay a per-mile charge (perhaps 25 cents per mile) when you return the vehicle. Any excess wear over the normal wear and tear is also your financial responsibility.

▼ **FIRST THINGS FIRST**
Federal law requires you receive cost information before you sign a lease.

 Review the dealer's warranty before you buy a vehicle. Check whether the manufacturer's warranty covers the lease term or the miles you can reasonably expect to drive under the lease.

NEGOTIABLE TERMS

You can negotiate:

- The agreed-upon value of the vehicle (if you negotiate a lower value, then your monthly payments will go down);
- The up-front payments, including the down payment;
- The length of the lease;
- The monthly lease payment;
- The end of lease payments, fees, and charges;
- The per year mileage and per-mile charge over the annual limit;
- The option to purchase at a specific price at the end of the lease;
- Insurance coverage, including coverage on lease payments if the vehicle is stolen or destroyed in an accident.

BUYING A USED VEHICLE

U sed car dealers are required to post a Buyers Guide but private people selling their own vehicles don't have to use the Buyers Guide.

BUYERS GUIDE

The Federal Trade Commission's Used Car Rule requires all used car dealers to post a one-page Buyers Guide in each car. It's intended to ensure that you get written information about warranties before you buy. The Buyers Guide must specify:

- If the vehicle is being sold "as is" or with a warranty (and, if so, whether the warranty is full or limited);
- Which systems are covered by the warranty and the time period of the warranty;
- If there's a limited warranty, the percentage of the parts and labor that the dealer will pay for when repairs are needed.

The Buyers Guide also advises you to ask the dealer to put all promises in writing and ask whether the car can be inspected by your mechanic on or off the lot.

The buyers guide becomes part of the sales contract and should be kept for future review. Any promises made by the salesperson must be written on the sales contract or buyers guide.

THINGS TO KNOW

- Dealers aren't required to give used car buyers a three-day cancellation period.
- The right to return a vehicle must be negotiated and written into the contract. Check with your dealer for more information on the return policy.
- Dealers may exchange a vehicle, give credit towards a higher priced vehicle, or simply offer you a cash refund.

ABOUT ODOMETERS

An odometer shows the number of miles a vehicle has been driven. As a result of concern about fraud in vehicle mileage readings, federal law requires the seller to write the odometer reading on the title and disclose whether the reading is the true mileage.

15 In many states, the law does not require an individual seller to offer a car that can pass state inspection.

TYPES OF WARRANTIES

There are different types of used vehicle warranties. You have a right to see a copy of the warranty from the dealer before you buy.

Warranty of merchantability. This is the most common type of implied warranty. It means the dealer promises that the car will run. It doesn't mean the dealer promises no future breakdowns. The warranty is breached if you can prove the problem existed at the time of the sale.

Warranty of fitness for a particular purpose. This means the dealer has promised that the vehicle will be suitable for a particular purpose. For example, the dealer tells you the vehicle has enough "horsepower" to haul your boat trailer and you purchased the vehicle based on this promise. If it breaks down while you're towing the trailer, then the repair should be covered under the warranty of fitness.

Full warranty. A full warranty means:
- During the warranty, you're entitled to warranty service;
- Warranty service is free;
- You can choose a replacement or full refund if the dealer can't repair the vehicle or a covered system.

If the dealer doesn't include these statements in the warranty, then you have a limited warranty.

Limited warranty. A limited warranty means you have costs, time restrictions, and coverage limitations. You may have to pay a deductible for a repair or for certain parts of the vehicle not fully covered.

As-is vehicle. An as-is vehicle is sold without any warranty. When you drive off the lot, the dealer has no further responsibility.

◀ **CAN YOU SELL IT "AS-IS?"**
Not all states allow "as-is" sales for used vehicles.

IT'S A FACT

The Federal Trade Commission reports that consumers buy 40 million used cars for $366 billion each year.

VEHICLE INSURANCE

J ust don't walk away at the end of an insurance policy or stop paying the premium during the term of the policy.

READING A POLICY

There are different types of coverages in an auto insurance policy:

- Bodily injury liability;
- Medical payments or personal injury protection;
- Property damage liability;
- Collision;
- Comprehensive;
- Uninsured/underinsured motorist.

With a few exceptions, states require some liability coverage. Liability coverage refers to insurance for damage you cause to another.

Those states requiring liability insurance set minimum amounts for certain coverages. The limits may be described in terms of three numbers. For example, 20/40/10 means the state requires $20,000 coverage for bodily injury per person; $40,000 coverage for bodily injury per accident; and $10,000 for property damage per accident.

YOUR CREDIT INFORMATION

Some companies may consider your credit rating in addition to your driving record when deciding whether to insure you. Some states restrict insurance companies' use of credit scores for auto insurance.

CANCELLATION OR NONRENEWAL

A cancellation or nonrenewal notice cutting off your vehicle insurance can be painful and frustrating. Each state has different rules and laws, so be sure to get proper advice.

- Cancellation means the company terminates your policy before it expires.
- Nonrenewal means the company refuses to renew your policy when it expires.

During the first 30 to 60 days (the binding period), the company may cancel for any lawful reason, including a ticket or an accident. If the company cancels you because of an accident, it still has to pay for damages covered by your policy.

If either you or the company cancels your policy, the company must refund premiums paid in advance that didn't buy coverage. This amount is called the "unearned premium." For example, if you paid a six-month premium of $600 and your policy was cancelled after one month, the company would owe you $500 in unearned premium.

There is no grace period for paying a car insurance premium. State laws will specify the number of days' notice that the insurer must provide before the cancellation is effective.

HOW DO I CANCEL MY POLICY?

You can probably cancel during the term of the policy by sending a written notice to the company. Check your policy.

At the end of the policy, you cannot just walk away. You must inform the insurance company that you are cancelling your policy. If you don't inform the company, you will be billed and, when you fail to pay, the company will cancel the policy. The company may inform a credit bureau and other companies may look at the cancellation as a negative factor in deciding whether to insure you.

ACCIDENT CHECKLIST

You might want to copy this and keep it in your glove box with your other documents.

- Move your vehicle out of traffic lanes to prevent further injury or damage;
- Call the police or highway patrol to report the accident;
- Get the other drivers(s) names, addresses, license numbers (including state), license plate number, color, make, year of all other vehicles, and proof of insurance from all other drivers;
- Get all witnesses' names, addresses, and telephone numbers;
- Note the weather conditions, time of day, light, and road conditions;
- Draw a map of the scene and record what you observed.
- Record the name, station, and badge number of all police officers. Ask for the accident number or where to call for the accident number later on;
- If your vehicle is towed from the scene, get the towing company's address, phone number; state license, and driver's name. If possible, find out the towing and storage charges and have your vehicle moved to the repair location as soon as possible;
- Notify your insurance company promptly. Mail the company any legal notices that you receive. Send only copies of documents and keep the originals for your file.

Repairing Vehicles

W*e all need to repair and service our vehicles. Here are some things to know about getting or taking your car to the shop.*

After an Accident

Depending on the state, you generally can decide where you want your vehicle repaired. You may have to provide up to three estimates to prove that your choice for repairs provided a reasonable estimate. Sometimes, an insurance company may have the final say. If the law requires the repair shop to be licensed, look for the certificate or ask to see it.

Source of parts. Insurance policies typically state that after a crash, the vehicle will be returned to its pre-accident state with parts that are of "like kind and quality." The issue is whether a car can be repaired with non-Original Equipment Manufacturer (OEM) parts. Non-OEM parts are sometimes called *after-market* parts and are cheaper than the manufacturer's parts.

Policies don't usually exclude OEM parts but you may need to insist on them if you want them. Depending on your policy, you may have to pay the difference in cost.

Most states have laws that address when and where insurers and auto body shops must disclose the use of non-OEM parts to consumers. In less than a dozen states, the law requires your approval before non-OEM parts can be used. In states that don't require insurers to tell you about non-OEM parts, you will have to be proactive and ask what's going into your car.

Warranty Coverage

Check your sales contract for your warranty coverage. If the vehicle is still covered under the manufacturer's warranty, you need to follow the rules to keep the warranty in effect.

If your warranty is still in effect, you probably will need to get the repair done at a dealer, even if it isn't the dealer who sold you the car. If you're travelling, call the local zone office of the manufacturer for the address of the closest dealer. This phone number is in your owner's manual. If you take the vehicle to an independent repair company, the manufacturer may not reimburse your expenses. You need permission usually in writing from the zone office, to take the vehicle to a non-franchised dealer or repair company.

Are You Getting Original Parts?

If your leased vehicle is in an accident, talk to your insurance company and dealer about whether your car will be repaired with OEM parts.

---

16 Be alert to whether manufacturer's parts or other parts are being used for repairs.

17 Check the box on the repair estimate to indicate you want the old parts returned to you.

TOWING

Here are some things to remember:

- Wait for an auto club or dealer-authorized towing truck. Some tow truck operators monitor auto club and police radios and attempt to pick up a vehicle before the called tow truck arrives. They're paid kick-backs from repair garages or will charge you an excessive amount for towing;

- Have the official tow truck take your vehicle where you want—either the dealer, your regular service company, or your home;

- If the truck takes your vehicle to a storage yard, you will incur storage costs and maybe another towing charge when you want the vehicle delivered.

GET AN ESTIMATE ▶
Before approving repairs, always check the car's warranty. Unless it's being serviced for warranty work, expect to get estimates and preapprove all work.

REPAIRS

There's no standard repair warranty. Be clear about what is covered by any warranty. After a mechanic has diagnosed the problem, you should receive a written estimate for the repair work. The estimate should include the vehicle description, mileage, service to be done, and an estimate of parts and labor. Salvage parts come from another vehicle and are seldom guaranteed.

UNRESOLVED ISSUES

If you have problems with repair service that can't be resolved through the manager, contact your state's consumer protection office. This office may be in the department of motor vehicles, state attorney general's office, department of insurance, or department of corporations and licensing. You can also contact the local Better Business Bureau to file a complaint.

CAR LEMON LAWS

L *emon laws are consumer protection laws that give car owners certain rights and remedies when a car can't be repaired.*

WHAT'S A LEMON?

If your vehicle has been repaired for the same problem a number of times, it may be considered a lemon. The basic element of a lemon law is that the manufacturer must replace the vehicle or refund the purchase price if after a certain number of repairs, the vehicle can't be repaired.

Since laws vary from state to state, here are some of the basic things to understand:

Know the law. For you to assert your rights under a state lemon law, you will need to meet the requirements of that state's law.

Used vehicles. The lemon law may apply to used vehicles as well as new.

Leased vehicles. The lemon law may apply to leased vehicles.

Motorcycles. Motorcycles generally aren't covered by the lemon law.

Motorhomes. Certain parts (for example, drive trains) may be covered;

Lawyers' fees. Some state laws allow a consumer who brings and wins a lemon lawsuit to recover attorney fees. Federal law allows recovery of attorney fees if you prevail in the lawsuit;

Limitations. States may have time or mileage limits, such as 12 to 24 months or 12,000 to 24,000 miles;

Serious defects. If the defect is a serious safety-related item, the manufacturer may be permitted one repair.

Safety defects. If the defect is not a serious but is a safety-related item, the manufacturer may be permitted two repairs.

Other defects. For other defects, the manufacturer may be permitted up to four repair attempts.

SOME DEALERS AND MANUFACTURERS AVOID LEMON LAWS

Here are some tactics to watch out for. The dealer or manufacturer might claim:

Fewer repairs. They may claim fewer repair attempts than needed to qualify under lemon laws;

Different parts. The repair orders may show different components so that a single component never failed more than once;

Minor issue. They may claim the problem is minor and won't affect use of the vehicle;

Your fault. You caused the problem. This excuse may include unauthorized repairs, abuse of the vehicle, or failure to perform the recommended scheduled maintenance.

WHO TO CONTACT

Disputes. For dispute resolution information, contact your local Better Business Bureau or automobile association.

Defects. Contact the National Highway Traffic Safety Administration. This federal agency has information on problems, repairs, and vehicle model histories. This information is useful when trying to prove that a vehicle model has a defect history.

Safety. Write to NHTSA, 400 Seventh St. SW, Washington, D.C. 20590 or call its Auto Safety Hotline at 888-DASH-2-DOT (888-327-4236) or go its website at http://www.nhtsa.dot.gov.

Any issues. Contact your state attorney general's office and ask for the consumer assistance department. Some states have separate consumer protection or automobile consumer protection departments.

ASSERTING YOUR RIGHTS

Good records. Keep a log of all phone calls, conversations, and contacts with the dealer's sales and service representatives. Note all the times, dates, and conditions that the symptoms or problems appear. Record the odometer reading and date when the car goes in for service.

Copies. Keep ORIGINAL copies of all correspondence with the dealer or manufacturer.

Written orders. When you leave your vehicle for service, insist on a formal written service order that details the symptoms, problems, and reference to previous service attempts.

Be skeptical. Do not accept the dealer's claim that they could not "duplicate the problem" or "the symptom is common with this model."

Guidelines. Follow the guidelines in your owners' manual for contacting the manufacturer.

OTHER RIGHTS AND RESOURCES

Consumers frequently ask about their
rights in these situations.

TELEPHONE RIGHTS

*Y ou need to be familiar with 900 numbers,
slamming, and cramming, to protect yourself.*

900 NUMBERS

A 900 number isn't a toll-free number. You pay for the
call. All print, radio, and television ads for 900
number services must include:

- The total flat fee cost or per minute rate, including any
  minimum and total cost if length of call is known;
- The range of fees if there are different rates,
  including the initial cost of the call and any
  minimum charges;
- The cost of any other 900 number to which you
  may be transferred;
- Any other fees charged.

An 800, 888, or other toll-free number can't connect
to a 900-number. You can't get a collect call back if
you dialed a toll-free number. If you don't want to
make 900-number calls, ask the phone company to
block them from your phone number.

WALDENBOOKS

LE   1897   103   7464   12-06-03
            REL 7.6/1.05   14   12:42:28

0789471736   6.95
            SUBTOTAL   6.95
N JERSEY 6.0% TAX   .42
            TOTAL   7.37
            CASH   7.37
            PV# 0037464

PREFERRED READERS SAVE EVERY DAY

========CUSTOMER RECEIPT=========

CRAMMING

Cramming means placing unauthorized or deceptive charges on your phone bill. These are for services you didn't order, authorize, or receive. Charges may be one-time or they may appear monthly.

Examples of items and services commonly charged to consumers include:

- Fees and service charges for additional phone services;
- Service fees for memberships, calling plans, contests;
- Minimum monthly fees or minimum usage fees.

THREE SECONDS

At the start of a 900 call costing more than $2, you should hear introductory information and have three seconds to hang up before you're charged.

18 Take the time to do your homework before selecting a provider, switching to another provider, and reviewing your bills.

SLAMMING

Slamming is an illegal practice of switching your long-distance phone company (carrier) without your approval. There can't be a switch unless you directly authorize it or authorize your new carrier to do it for you. To protect yourself from slamming:

- You can "freeze" your existing carrier to prevent another carrier from claiming it had permission to change your carrier;
- Don't deposit "checks" from long distance companies because signing and depositing them may give your written permission to switch phone carriers;
- If you receive a letter or postcard verifying that you've switched carriers, contact the party and state that you didn't authorize the change. Call your authorized long-distance carrier to confirm that your account is still active;
- If you notice billing from a new phone carrier, call the carrier's 800 number and say that you didn't order service. Call your local phone company and tell them to reconnect you to your authorized (old) carrier and you want any reconnection charges taken off your bill. Call your authorized long distance carrier to report the switch and ask to be reconnected at no cost to you.

If you catch the illegal switch and report it, you must be told that you're not required to pay charges for the first 30 days. If you've already paid before you notice you were switched without permission, the unauthorized carrier must forward your payments to the authorized carrier and issue a refund for any amount in excess of what you would have paid that carrier.

FUNERAL RIGHTS

W*hen you've lost a loved one, the family member who must decide about funeral services and cremation is a particularly vulnerable consumer. Consumers are entitled to information before making any decisions.*

OPTIONS

Traditional full-service. This type of funeral means that there is a viewing or visitation, use of a hearse to transport the body to the cemetery, burial, and entombment or cremation of the remains. Costs also include the funeral home's basic fee, embalming and dressing the body, rental of the funeral home for the viewing, and rental of the vehicles to transport the family. The casket and cemetery plot or crypt are added costs.

Direct burial. This is a burial shortly after death, without embalming, in a simple container.

Direct cremation. This type of service occurs shortly after death without embalming.

EMBALMING

Embalming is generally not required by law and the Funeral Rule prohibits the funeral provider from falsely telling you that it is. Embalming may be necessary if there is a viewing. You must be told in writing that you can choose cremation or direct burial that doesn't require embalming.

BASIC SERVICES

A funeral provider can charge a standard fee for basic services that apply to all funerals, regardless of the specific arrangements. You can't decline to pay this fee if you select that provider. Basic services usually include funeral planning, permits and death certificates, notices, sheltering the remains, and coordinating the arrangements.

> **19** The FTC's Funeral Rule prohibits claims that certain caskets, features on a casket, or processes, such as embalming, can preserve the body indefinitely.

58

VETERANS BENEFITS

Veterans are entitled to be buried in a national cemetery with a grave marker without charge. The Department of Veterans Affairs can provide information. Your state may also have veteran cemeteries and you should contact your state for eligibility information.

PREPAYMENTS

For those who prepay funerals or expenses, state laws may prescribe how the funeral home or cemetery maintain the funds. For example, some state laws may require that part of the prepayment funds be placed in a trust or used for life insurance policies with the death benefits assigned to the funeral home or cemetery.

DISCLOSURES BEFORE PURCHASING

Under the Funeral Rule, enforced by the Federal Trade Commission, you're entitled to receive itemized prices. You must also be told you have the right to choose the goods and services that you want (with some exceptions) and to receive your choices in writing on the price list. The law doesn't prohibit "funeral packages," but you must be shown an itemized price list.

Pre-showing. Before showing you caskets, funeral providers must show you a description and price list. This rule is based on research showing consumers typically buy one of the first three caskets they're shown.

Off-premise purchase. If you purchased a casket elsewhere, a funeral provider may not refuse to handle it or charge a fee.

Cremation. If you select cremation, the funeral provider must offer various alternative containers.

Required items. If the law requires a specific item, it must be stated on your price list along with a reference to the specific law.

Markups. You must be told in writing about any markup fees (but not the amount of the markup) for items the funeral provider must buy.

In Deepest Sympathy

20 A traditional funeral costs in the thousands of dollars and, with all the other items added in, may cost more than $10,000.

HEALTHCARE RIGHTS

*P*atient rights are based on informed consent. Patients should use that principle to empower them in healthcare decisions.

PATIENT RIGHTS

You have the right to know all relevant information about your treatment and give informed consent to accept or refuse it. You may sign a form when you enter a healthcare facility that has a consent component to it.

Advanced directives. Under the Patient Self-Determination Act, patients entering a healthcare facility that receives Medicare or Medicaid funds must receive information on "advance directives." Advance directives include a:

- Living will, which addresses whether to withhold or withdraw life-sustaining treatment if you can't communicate your wishes;
- Healthcare power of attorney, which gives another person the authority to make medical decisions if you can't make them.

Your medical record should include whether you signed an advance directive. You don't, however, need an advance directive. A healthcare facility can't deny you admission because you don't have one. You can change your advance directive as long as you can communicate your wishes.

MEDICARE RIGHTS

You have the right to information, which includes handbooks and other publications about coverage. You also have the right to choose and switch between original Medicare and other Medicare plans. In coming years, you can expect to be limited to a particular timeframe for switching.

If you want to buy supplemental coverage (known as Medigap), you have the right to do so. You can't be turned down for Medigap coverage if you buy a policy within six months of enrolling in Medicare Part B. But after that period, the company isn't required to insure you and may deny you coverage based on your health.

If you're denied a service or told that you must pay for a service not covered by Medicare, and you get the denial in writing, you can file an appeal. Because the process is different for original Medicare and private plans, be sure to look at your handbook and check with your state health insurance assistance program.

NURSING HOME RIGHTS

The Nursing Home Reform Law, a federal law, covers nursing homes that receive Medicare or Medicaid and applies to patients whether or not they receive Medicare or Medicaid.

Under the federal law, for example, nursing homes that receive Medicare or Medicaid:

- Can't deny a resident the right to see family, an ombudsman or advocate, physicians, or state or federal government representatives;
- Can't ask a resident to leave because s/he is receiving federal benefits;
- Must give equal access to care regardless of whether the resident is paying privately or receiving federal benefits;
- Must provide a list of charges for services that aren't covered;
- Can't restrain or abuse residents to punish them;
- Must provide a notice of a resident's rights at admission;
- Can't require residents to place their personal monies with the facility.

INFORMATION ABOUT YOUR PROVIDER

To find information about your doctor, you can contact:

- Your state licensing board for licensing information and public discipline actions;
- The American Medical Association for information on training and certification;
- The American Board of Medical Specialties for information on specialty board certification;
- Internet websites that contain a range of information including disciplinary actions. Some may charge a fee.

The U.S. Department of Health and Human Services operates the National Practitioner Data Bank (NPDB) and The Healthcare Integrity and Protection Data Bank (HIPDB). These databases collect information about professional competence, such as adverse actions regarding licensure and certification, exclusions from participation in government programs, convictions, and civil judgments. Consumers, however, aren't allowed to obtain information from these databases. Consumers must rely primarily on public record information from their state licensing board and court records.

GOVERNMENT SERVICES AND INFORMATION

Y ou may think of government only in terms of your obligations, such as taxes and licenses. As a consumer of government services, though, you have the right to information on many topics.

FREEDOM OF INFORMATION ACT

The Freedom of Information Act (FOIA) requires the federal government to disclose records (subject to certain exemptions and exclusions) upon your written request. FOIA applies only to federal agencies and doesn't give you the right to obtain records from Congress, the courts, or state and local governments.

Each federal agency is responsible for its own records and responding to requests. If you need information from several agencies, you will need to make a request to each one.

Many states also have laws covering access to public records. To obtain state and local government records, you need to follow the provisions of your state's laws.

▲ EXPENSIVE TOOLS
In the 1980s, Congress acted in response to public outcries over the fact that private contractors were charging the Pentagon exorbitant fees for everyday items. This hammer is one example.

WHISTLEBLOWER PROTECTION

Federal laws protect whistleblowers in specific matters. In addition, most states have whistleblower statutes that generally protect employees from discrimination based on their reports of fraud in government. The provisions vary from state to state but the concept behind these kinds of laws is to ensure that complainants receive protection.

21 The U.S. Department of Justice has a list of principal FOIA contacts at federal agencies at its website.

FALSE CLAIMS

The False Claims Act was enacted during the Civil War to protect the government from unscrupulous supply contractors. In 1986, in response to concerns about contractor fraud, Congress passed an amendment to the Act, giving citizens an incentive to take action if they have information about fraudulent claims to the federal government.

The law allows a private citizen—a present or former employee, competitor, a patient, or anyone—who has knowledge about a false claim paid by the government to file a lawsuit on behalf of the United States. The person who files the suit (a qui tam) is called a relator and may recover between 15% and 30% of any settlement or judgment. Under the False Claims Act, a company faces penalties of up to three times the damages plus $5,000 to $10,000 for each false claim An example would be to allege that a company submitted false claims for lab test results for a Medicare patient.

IT'S A FACT

Since 1986, more than 3,000 lawsuits have been brought and more than $3 billion have been recovered under the False Claims Act. The federal government has paid more than $550 million to whistleblowers under this law.

THE ROLE OF INSPECTORS GENERAL

In 1978, Congress passed the Inspector General Act to create independent watchdogs for federal government agencies. The purpose of the law is to promote economy and efficiency in government agencies and prevent and detect fraud in programs and operations. The law gave inspectors general broad access to their agencies' documents and information.

Today, there are more than 60 inspectors general in federal agencies. The inspectors general have audit and investigatory functions and report their activities to Congress semiannually. Citizens can report allegations of fraud, waste, abuse, or misconduct in government agencies to the appropriate federal agency's inspector general.

Employees are protected from reprisals for making a complaint to an inspector general except in cases known to be false or with a willful disregard for the truth.

Some states have statewide inspectors general, and others have inspectors general for specific agencies. If you have a complaint about how your state government is doing its job, check your phonebook, or contact your representative or state attorney general's office to see whether there's an inspector general who oversees that function.

EMPLOYMENT RIGHTS

E mployment rights can encompass a broad range of topics. Often applicants are concerned about background investigations and what the employer can find out about them.

EMPLOYMENT BACKGROUND INVESTIGATIONS

Background checks help employers determine the accuracy and completeness of information provided by applicants.

Types of information. Laws may limit the use of certain applicant information by employers.

Education laws. These laws may also restrict certain education information, such as transcripts, disciplinary records, and financial records, without the student's permission. Basic information, however, such as dates of attendance and degrees, may be released without permission.

Fair questions. Questions about age, marital status, and certain other areas may not be permitted in job interviews.

Former work. In practice, most employers are only providing limited information about former employees. For example, they often only confirm employment dates and final salary.

Credit checks. Prospective employers must tell job applicants if they intend to obtain a consumer report, and the applicant must consent in writing prior to the credit check. If the employer uses the report to deny the job, the employer must provide a copy of the report and notice that the applicant can dispute the information in the report.

RECORDS

Employers may want to receive the following information:

- Driving records;
- Criminal and court records;
- References;
- Property ownership;
- Licensing records;
- Social Security number;
- Prior employment;
- Education;
- Bankruptcy;
- Credit records;
- Military service records.

SEXUAL HARASSMENT

Under Title VII of the Civil Rights Act of 1964, sexual harassment is prohibited in the workplace. Prohibited conduct includes unwelcome sexual advances or requests for sexual favors when it "explicitly or implicitly affects an individual's employment, unreasonably interferes with an individual's work performance or creates an intimidating, hostile, or offensive work environment." The harasser and victim may be either male or female. The harasser could be a supervisor or co-worker. The victim doesn't have to have economic injury. Most important, however, the harasser's conduct must be unwelcome to the victim.

DISABLED EMPLOYEES

Employers must "provide a reasonable accommodation to a qualified applicant or employee with a disability" unless it would pose an "undue hardship" on the employer. Examples of reasonable accommodations are modifying equipment, restructuring a job, part-time or modified work schedules, and providing interpreters. The applicant or employee usually has the responsibility to inform the employer about the need for a reasonable accommodation.

AMERICANS WITH DISABILITIES ACT

The Americans with Disabilities Act of 1990 (ADA) protects those defined as having "a physical or mental impairment that substantially limits one or more major life activities" from discrimination in employment, housing, education, state and local government activities, and access to public transportation and public accommodations. The ADA applies to:

● Private employers with more than 15 employees;
● State and local governments with more than 15 employees;
● Employment agencies;
● Labor organizations;
● Labor-management committees.

The U.S. Equal Employment Opportunity Commission and local civil rights agencies enforce the ADA against employers who discriminate against qualified disabled applicants and employees.

DANGEROUS PRODUCTS AND RECALLS

W*hen an item has been linked to health or safety problems, the item may be recalled by the seller or manufacturer to protect consumers.*

VEHICLES AND EQUIPMENT

Under the National Traffic and Motor Vehicle Safety Act, the National Highway Traffic Safety Administration (NHTSA) is authorized to:

● Issue minimum performance standards for vehicle safety and occupant protection in the event of a crash;

● Require manufacturers to issue recalls of vehicles with safety defects.

The NHTSA's responsibilities for occupant protection include seat belts, child safety seats, and airbags.

Manufacturer roles. The manufacturer is responsible for notifying the NHTSA, vehicle owners, dealers, and distributors of a safety defect. To fix a recalled item, the manufacturer can repair or replace it at no charge, or provide a refund.

Based on the Firestone tire recall and its related hearings in 2000, a new law was passed by Congress. To help avoid problems such as those involved with the Firestone tires, this legislation requires manufacturers to report safety problems in foreign countries and provide early warning information (such as claims data) to NHTSA. In addition, the legislation calls for improved tire labeling.

IT'S A FACT

Since 1966, the NHTSA has overseen recalls of more than 200 million cars, trucks, and other vehicles.

RESOURCES

National Highway Traffic Safety Administration (www.nhtsa.dot.gov) Their Auto Safety Hotline is 888-327-4236. Call to report a safety defect, get recall information, or obtain publications.

U.S. Department of Agriculture, Food Safety and Inspection Service (www.fsis.usda.gov) They're responsible for domestic and imported meat, poultry, and egg products. The Meat and Poultry Hotline is 800-535-4555.

U.S. Consumer Product Safety Commission (www.cpsc.gov) They protect the public from product-related injuries. To report a problem or obtain recall information, call 800-638-2772.

U.S. Food and Drug Administration (www.fda.gov) They oversee domestic and imported food (except for meat and poultry) and drugs. Call 888-INFO-FDA.

CONSUMER PRODUCTS

The Consumer Product Safety Commission (CPSC) is an independent federal regulatory agency with jurisdiction over 15,000 consumer products. Its purpose is to:

- Protect the public from unsafe products;
- Provide information to assess product safety;
- Develop uniform safety standards;
- Promote research and investigation into product-related injuries.

The CPSC develops voluntary and mandatory standards for industries, obtains product recalls, conducts research on potential product hazards, and informs and educates the public.

NON-MEAT AND DRUGS

The Food and Drug Administration (FDA) has responsibility for:

- Seafood;
- Fruits, vegetables, and other non-meat products;
- Bottled water;
- Dietary supplements.

The FDA ensures the safety of medical devices, medicines, and biologics (including insulin and vaccines).

Recall information is available on each agency's websites.

MEAT, POULTRY, AND EGG PRODUCTS

The Department of Agriculture is responsible for the safety of meat, poultry, and egg products as well as for correct labeling and packaging. Food Safety and Inspection Service (FSIS) responds to concerns about meat or poultry products that may be adulterated (a risk to health or unfit for consumption) or misbranded (bad labeling or packaging).

All recalls are voluntary but the FSIS has the authority to seize the product for consumer safety. The FSIS also is responsible for notifying the public about meat and poultry recalls.

If you have a concern about restaurant food, contact your local health department.

RESOURCES

C onsumer help is available from federal and state government agencies and many consumer advocacy groups. Because consumer rights often spring from a grass-roots project, you may even need to speak up yourself or form a group to fight for your rights. Here are some resources to begin.

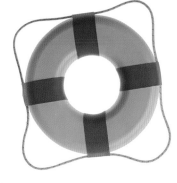

AARP

(www.aarp.org) The American Association of Retired Persons is dedicated to the issues relevant to people 50 years of age and older; 800-424-3410.

ACLU

(www.aclu.org) The American Civil Liberties Union focuses on issues affecting individual freedom. To contact them, call a local ACLU office listed in your telephone directory.

ATTORNEYS GENERAL

(www.naag.org) If you have a consumer issue involving the laws of your state, contact your state attorney general. Find links to all state attorneys general at the association's website.

BBB

(www.bbb.org) The Council of Better Business Bureaus has more than 100 local offices nationwide. Check out a business or find out about the dispute resolution program. Check your telephone directory for the nearest BBB.

FCC

(www.fcc.gov) The Federal Ccommunications Commission oversees interstate and international communications by radio, television, wire, satellite and cable. To make a complaint or obtain information, call 888-CALL-FCC.

FTC

(www.ftc.gov) The Federal Trade Commission is responsible for enforcing numerous consumer protection laws focusing on deceptive and unfair trade practices. To file a complaint or obtain information, call 877-FTC-HELP (877-382-4357).

HUD

(www.hud.gov) The U.S. Department of Housing and Urban Development is responsible for handling complaints regarding housing discrimination, manufactured housing, and land sales. Call 202-708-1112.

INSURE.COM

(www.insure.com) They provide consumer information and resources on life, health, annuities, car, and home insurance topics.

NAIC

(www.naic.org) National Assocation of Insurance Commissioners has insurance regulators' names and addresses for each state and information on state health insurance contacts.

NARUC

(www.naruc.org) The National Association of Regulatory Utility Commissioners will link you to your state public utility commission.

CREDIT REPORTING AGENCIES

Equifax. www.equifax.com; 800-685-1111;

Experian. www.experian.com; 888-EXPERIAN (397-3742);

Trans Union. www.transunion.com; 800-888-4213.

NASUCA

(www.nasuca.org) National Association of State Utility Consumer Advocates is an association of state utility consumer advocate offices.

NOLO.COM

Nolo provides self-help for consumers on a wide array of consumer topics; 800-728-3555.

PUBLIC CITIZEN

(www.citizen.org) Founded by Ralph Nader, Public Citizen is a consumer advocacy organization that promotes consumer interests in energy, environment, trade, health, and government issues; 202-588-1000.

OTHER SITES

Here are some other websites to know:

- www.firstgov.gov (portal to all federal government information);
- www.consumer.gov (food, product safety, money, children, transportation and other topics);
- www.foodsafety.gov (food safety information);
- www.healthfinder.gov (consumer health information);
- www.afterschool.gov (for kids sites).

INDEX

ACKNOWLEDGMENTS

AUTHORS' ACKNOWLEDGMENTS

The production of this book has called on the skills of many people. We would particularly like to thank our editors at Dorling Kindersley, and our consultant, Nick Clemente. Marc wishes to dedicate this book to Zachary Robinson for his great patience and support when it was most needed. Special thanks to Teresa Clavasquin for her generous support and assistance.

PUBLISHER'S ACKNOWLEDGMENTS

Dorling Kindersley would like to thank everyone who worked on the Essential Finance series, and the following for their help and participation:

Editorial Stephanie Rubenstein; **Design and Layout** Jill Dupont; **Consultants** Nick Clemente; Skeeter; **Indexer** Rachel Rice; **Proofreader** Stephanie Rubenstein; **Photography** Anthony Nex; **Photographers' Assistants** Howard Linton; **Models** Bud Lieberman, Ashley Dupont, Debra Armstrong, Darby Wilson, Alexandra Romano, Tom Dupont, Stephanie Rose; **Picture Researcher** Mark Dennis; Sam Ruston

AUTHOR'S BIOGRAPHIES

Nicolette Parisi, Ph.D., J.D., is a consumer rights consultant and writes on consumer issues for About.com. From 1995 to 1999, Parisi was the Pennsylvania Inspector General. During her career, she has practiced in the litigation department of a large law firm, taught college-level criminal justice courses, conducted research on criminal justice topics, and worked for state government investigating fraud, waste, and misconduct. Her Ph.D. in criminal justice is from the State University of New York at Albany and her J.D. is from Temple University School of Law in Philadelphia.

Marc Robinson is co-founder of Internet-based moneytours.com, a personal finance resource for corporations, universities, credit unions, and other institutions interested in helping their constituents make intelligent decisions about their financial lives. He wrote the original *The Wall Street Journal Guide to Understanding Money and Markets*, created *The Wall Street Journal Guide to Understanding Personal Finance*, co-published a personal finance series with Time Life Books, and wrote a children's book about onomateopia in different languages. In his two decades in the financial services industry, Marc has provided marketing consulting to many top Wall Street firms. He is admitted to practice law in New York State.